THE PAT RILEY EFFECT

How One Man Changed Basketball

CHARLES HERRON

Copyright @ 2024 By Charles Herron

All rights reserved. No part of this book may be reproduced, distributed, or transmitted in any form or by any means, including photocopying, recording, or other electronic or mechanical methods, without the prior written permission of the publisher, except in the case of brief quotations embodied in critical reviews and specific other noncommercial uses permitted by copyright law.

Contents

INTRODUCTION

The Riley Effect

CHAPTER 1: FROM PLAYER TO COACH

Pat Riley's early years, his playing days, and his transition to coaching

CHAPTER 2: SHOWTIME LAKERS – BUILDING A DYNASTY

The beginning of the "Showtime" era with the Los Angeles Lakers and the making of a championship team

CHAPTER 3: THE ART OF WINNING

Riley's unique coaching style, motivational techniques, and his philosophy on building winning teams

CHAPTER 4: A NEW CHALLENGE – THE NEW YORK KNICKS

How Riley transformed the Knicks into contenders and embraced a tougher, defensive style

CHAPTER 5: MIAMI HEAT – MORE THAN JUST A COACH

Riley's transition to the Miami Heat, from head coach to team president, and his vision for the franchise

CHAPTER 6: HEAT CULTURE – A LEGACY OF DISCIPLINE

Exploring the "Heat Culture" that Riley established, emphasizing discipline, resilience, and teamwork

CHAPTER 7: THE BIG THREE ERA

The formation of Miami's "Big Three" with LeBron James, Dwyane Wade, and Chris Bosh, and the pursuit of championships

CHAPTER 8: LEADERSHIP BEYOND THE COURT

Riley's impact as a mentor, team builder, and innovator within the NBA

CHAPTER 9: THE RILEY PLAYBOOK – LESSONS IN SUCCESS AND RESILIENCE

Life lessons and core principles from Riley's playbook on leadership and success

CHAPTER 10: THE LASTING LEGACY OF PAT RILEY

How Riley's impact is still felt across the league and his enduring influence on the sport

CONCLUSION

A Game Visionary

INTRODUCTION

The Riley Effect

Based on the most exciting events in basketball history, Pat Riley's life narrative reads like a legend. As a formidable player, a famous coach, and a brilliant executive, Riley has commanded the court from every perspective. He is a towering figure in both personality and physical presence. He has mastered the art of winning, molded some of the NBA's most recognizable teams, and left a legacy that is as unwavering as the man himself.

Riley's path is one of ongoing change for everyone involved, including himself. A competitive fire that would later define him drove him early in life while he was growing up in upstate New York. By the time he made it to the NBA, his rough, unyielding style of play reflected his no-nonsense outlook on life. Riley soon discovered, however, that his full potential extended beyond the court. He was destined to become the mastermind behind the game, directing plays from the sidelines and pushing players to reach previously unimaginable heights of performance.

His first significant influence was with the Los Angeles Lakers, a squad that would later become the pinnacle of domination, speed, and style. Riley became the Lakers' iconic "Showtime" team when he took over as head coach in the early 1980s. The Lakers represented Riley's vision of basketball as entertainment and art in motion, going beyond simply being a high-scoring force. Riley built a squad with players like Magic Johnson, Kareem Abdul-Jabbar, and James Worthy, who not only won games but also won over supporters all over the world. But beyond Showtime's glitter and glamor was an unwavering determination. Riley pushed his players to perform not just for the scoreboard but also for the history books because he wanted perfection. The Lakers won four titles under his direction in the 1980s and established the benchmark for what a basketball dynasty could be.

Riley's years with the New York Knicks, however, demonstrated his tough, streetwise edge if "Showtime" represented the glitzy side of his career. After leaving Los Angeles, Riley took on a squad that was having trouble defining itself and transformed them into the strong, brave, and unreservedly competitive person he was. Riley brought a new style of play to the Knicks, one that was characterized by a gritty mentality, a hard-nosed defense, and a readiness to fight. This team was founded on ferocity rather than skill. Riley's team, the Knicks, were known for their ability to shut down opponents and make every possession a battle of will. He made a lasting impression and cemented his image as a coach who could shape any squad to suit his vision, even though he never brought a championship to New York. Riley's versatility, his ability to evaluate both skill and temperament and his ability to shape each player into a vital component of a coherent, unstoppable force were all demonstrated by the Knicks.

However, Riley's tale goes beyond teaching. He changed again as he moved from the court to the front office, becoming an executive who would create a franchise culture rather than just teams. His transfer to the Miami Heat in the middle of the 1990s signaled the start of the "Heat Culture," a phrase that has come to represent perseverance, discipline, and the unwavering pursuit of greatness. Riley transformed a young squad into a consistent competitor by bringing his all-in attitude to Miami. And he accomplished it with the same unwavering vision, establishing guidelines that would influence the company for many years to come. Riley established a culture that valued diligence, responsibility, and, most importantly, the quest for success, thanks to his painstaking attention to detail and brutal work ethic.

Riley oversaw the Miami Heat's transformation from an expansion team to a dominant force, and in 2006, with Riley once again serving as coach, they won their first NBA championship. Shaquille O'Neal and later the renowned "Big Three" of LeBron James, Dwyane Wade, and Chris Bosh were drawn to the team because of his leadership. These players' entrance was more than just a recruiting success; it was the realization of Riley's ambitious goal of assembling a group of elite athletes dedicated to winning titles. Riley's status as one of the most prosperous sports executives was cemented in 2012 and 2013 when Miami won back-to-back titles under the "Big Three" era.

But Riley's ring collection and star-studded lineups aren't the only things that make him genuinely remarkable. He can adjust and change with the game and motivate everyone around him to follow suit. Riley has a remarkable capacity to observe the game from every perspective, comprehending its changes and modifying his strategy to stay ahead, whether he is coaching on the sidelines or planning from the boardroom. His mind functions as a chessboard, with every move being strategic and every player representing a piece in the bigger picture of winning.

Riley's real legacy is found in the culture he has fostered, the innumerable players he has coached, and the high standards he has established for both himself and his teams—beyond the titles and honors. Riley is well-known for saying things like "the disease of more," which cautions against complacency, and "no rebounds, no rings." His wisdom extends beyond basketball and is based on discipline, attention, and an unwavering quest for greatness. The Heat still bear his mark and uphold the principles he taught. "Heat Culture" is more than just a catchphrase in Miami; it's the way of life.

You'll explore Pat Riley's many facets as you read these pages—player, coach, executive, and leader. Discover his career-defining ideas, tactics, and mental toughness, as well as the development of a man who, despite his achievements, never stopped pushing and innovating. Few people have ever altered basketball like Pat Riley, and his impact is just as strong now as it was when he first took the floor. This is the tale of 'The Pat Riley Effect', a history of perseverance, success, and a relentless will to succeed.

CHAPTER 1: FROM PLAYER TO COACH

Pat Riley's early years, his playing days, and his transition to coaching

The narrative of Pat Riley starts in the hard-working town of Schenectady, New York, where street corners and basketball courts were used as trial runs for young people with lofty goals. Riley was born on March 20, 1945, and was raised in a competitive household. His father, Leon Riley, was a hardy, diligent man who played baseball in the minor leagues and spent years traveling across America to pursue his own goals. Young Pat learnt from his father that achieving greatness wasn't a pleasant journey; rather, it was hard, unrelenting, and required sacrifice. As Riley watched his father persevere through setback after setback while pursuing his passion, he learnt perseverance skills that would eventually shape his career.

Riley was more than just a regular student at school; he was an athlete who seemed destined to play. He became a multisport sensation at Linton High School, drawing attention with his intense will to succeed, his physicality, and his strong resolve. He excelled on the basketball floor and football pitch because of his fierce competitive spirit. But he discovered his real calling in basketball. Although he wasn't the tallest or most visually striking athlete, he had a talent for exceeding his limitations, motivating teammates, and performing well under pressure. Coaches noted his perseverance and exceptional ability to command respect on the court.

He still needed to show himself to the world, even if his coaches and family believed he had something unique. That chance arrived in 1963 when the renowned Adolph Rupp of the University of Kentucky recruited him to play. Rupp was a coach who would not accept anything short of perfection, and Kentucky basketball was as popular as it got in collegiate athletics. Riley gained a completely new level of discipline here. Rupp expected his players to perform at the highest level both on the court and in their demeanor. Riley flourished despite the demanding and occasionally harsh environment, putting his all into sessions, watching game recordings, and playing every game.

Riley was a team leader and a favorite among the fans at Kentucky because of his toughness and drive. In a momentous clash that would forever alter collegiate basketball, he guided the Wildcats to the NCAA Championship game in his junior year, when they met Texas Western. Riley's Kentucky team, which had an all-white roster that represented a sharply divided era, was the complete opposite of Texas Western, which had an all-Black starting lineup. Riley left the game knowing more about the significance of athletics than wins and loses, even if Kentucky lost in the end. He learnt from that game how the court could serve as a platform for something greater than the game itself—something that opened his eyes, broke conventions, and defied expectations.

He was a tough, competitive athlete by the time he graduated from college, but he was also a young man who had been shaped by discipline, adversity, and a strong sense of purpose. Although he was aware that the road ahead would not be simple, his upbringing had adequately equipped him. They laid the groundwork for his illustrious career by providing him with the mental toughness, tenacity, and unwavering work ethic that would take him from the slums of Schenectady to the epicenter of the basketball world.

The compelling story of Pat Riley's transition from player to coach is interwoven with his on-court experiences and his unwavering drive to revolutionize basketball. Riley was born in Schenectady, New York, on March 20, 1945. Growing up in a competitive family with a father who played minor-league baseball, he became passionate about sports at a young age. As a multisport athlete, he was particularly good at basketball and attracted scouts' notice at Linton High School. His future success was paved with his dedication to hard work and perseverance, which brought him to the University of Kentucky, where he played for the renowned coach Adolph Rupp.

Riley developed his abilities and learnt the tactical nuances of the game at Kentucky, where he flourished in a disciplined and competitive environment. He participated in the Wildcats' deep runs in the NCAA tournament and played with future NBA players. He was a respected player by the time he graduated in 1967, but making the switch to the professional league would present a different set of difficulties.

He joined a league very different from collegiate basketball when he was chosen by the San Diego Rockets with the seventh overall pick in the 1967 NBA Draft. He soon learnt that the NBA was full of exceptionally gifted athletes, many of them bigger and quicker than anyone he had ever encountered. Riley struggled to establish himself throughout his freshman season. Although he showed glimpses of promise, he needed to improve with consistency, scoring only 6.7 points per game for the youthful, rebuilding Rockets.

Riley's career would take a different turn when he was traded to the Los Angeles Lakers after just one season in San Diego. The Lakers were a legendary team with a devoted following and several Hall of Famers. Riley discovered a better setting where he could hone his abilities under coach Joe Mullaney. Riley saw what it was like to be a part of a winning culture while playing with such greats as Wilt Chamberlain, Elgin Baylor, and Jerry West. He earned a spot in the Lakers' rotation thanks to his reputation for playing strong defense and making clutch plays.

His career reached its zenith in the early 1970s when he was instrumental in the team's triumph. Riley played an important part in the Lakers' remarkable run to the NBA Championship in 1972. As he watched Coach Bill Sharman plan the team's offensive and defensive plans, he not only contributed as a player but also started to grasp the subtleties of coaching and strategy.

Riley played for seven years and retired in 1976 with respectable stats: 11 points, 4.3 rebounds, and 3.2 assists per game on average. He had little trouble making the switch from player to coach. Even though he was giving up playing, his passion for the game persisted. He received a fresh perspective on basketball when he accepted a broadcasting position with the Lakers shortly after retiring. Riley furthered his knowledge of the sport by analyzing games from the sidelines while working as a color commentator. He developed an analytical approach that would become a defining characteristic of his coaching style by researching offensive tactics, defensive settings, and player movements.

The Lakers encountered an unforeseen circumstance in 1979 when they required a new head coach. After hiring Paul Westhead, the club struggled to settle into a routine as the season went on. The Lakers hired Riley as an assistant coach to take over after Westhead was dismissed halfway through the 1979–80 campaign. Riley's illustrious coaching career would begin with this moment.

Riley made a seamless transition from commentator to head coach despite the fact that taking over in the middle of the season is always challenging. He eagerly seized the chance, eager to put his team's concept into action. Riley recognised the potential for greatness in a squad full of talented players, such as James Worthy, Kareem Abdul-Jabbar, and a youthful Magic Johnson. Using a fast-paced approach that capitalized on the team's skill and agility, he started to develop a new philosophy of play that would later be known as "Showtime."

The Lakers established a fast-paced, high-scoring strategy under Riley's direction, depending on spectacular plays and seamless transitions. The squad thrived, finishing the season with a 60-22 record after winning 30 of their final 46 games. Riley really established himself during the Lakers' matchup against the Philadelphia 76ers in the 1980 NBA Finals. Riley took a risk in Game 6 by starting Magic Johnson at centre, a position he had never played previously, in a crucial championship game when Abdul-Jabbar was out by injury. Johnson's talent and adaptability enabled the Lakers to win in a dramatic game and win their first title since 1972.

Riley's legendary coaching career began with his accomplishment in the inaugural season. He would go on to become one of the best coaches in NBA history by leading the Lakers to four more titles in the 1980s. His playing career established the groundwork for his strategic thinking, ability to inspire teammates, and unwavering drive for excellence.

CHAPTER 2: SHOWTIME LAKERS – BUILDING A DYNASTY

The beginning of the "Showtime" era with the Los Angeles Lakers and the making of a championship team

A fascinating period in professional basketball history, the Los Angeles Lakers debut of the "Showtime" era was characterized by creativity, thrills, and a dynamic style of play that enthralled spectators everywhere. The Lakers became one of the greatest teams in sports history as a result of this metamorphosis, which started in the late 1970s and reached its zenith in the 1980s. Pat Riley was at the center of this movement because he saw the potential in his great roster and realized that a change in mindset was required to play to their strengths.

When the Lakers chose Magic Johnson as the first overall pick in the 1979 NBA Draft, the groundwork for Showtime was established. Johnson, who was 6 feet 9 inches tall, was a remarkable player who could play a variety of positions. He was a perfect fit for the Lakers' style because of his special skill set, which included outstanding passing skills, court vision, and basketball IQ. Even though the club already had well-known players like Kareem Abdul-Jabbar, Magic's entrance was a game-changer. With a fast-paced, high-scoring style of play, the Lakers required a new strategy that would not only make use of their current talent but also attract new supporters.

After taking over as head coach halfway through the previous season, Pat Riley realized he needed to put in place a system that encouraged spontaneity and innovation in order to bring out the best in his players. In his ideal game, highlight-reel plays and quick breaks would be the rule rather than the exception. The players were excited to introduce a unique style of basketball to

Los Angeles, and they enthusiastically accepted this concept. Riley's leadership played a key role in this change; his strong emphasis on discipline, training, and teamwork inspired players to push themselves to the limit and rethink their positions on the court.

The Lakers changed their style of play to emphasize pace and ball movement as the 1980 season began. By taking advantage of fast breaks and generating scoring opportunities before opponents could deploy their defenses, the team's transition game became deadly. A potent combination was created by Magic Johnson's ability to create plays and Kareem Abdul-Jabbar's commanding presence on the court. Abdul-Jabbar's skyhook remained an unstoppable offensive weapon, while Johnson's ability to push the ball up the court and find open teammates became a hallmark of the Showtime era.

The players' chemistry grew stronger as the season went on. Every match was a display of skill and style that attracted spectators looking for a show. The Lakers gained notoriety for their ability to score in transition, which frequently resulted in spectacular alley-oops and dunks. Basketball fans were treated to a thrilling and successful style of the game. The group soon began winning, proving that Riley's goal was a real thing rather than just a pipe dream.

The 1980 NBA Finals matchup with the Philadelphia 76ers was one of the pivotal events of the Showtime era. Two of the league's most illustrious teams faced off in this final series, which also featured a collision of opposing styles. The 76ers featured a more conventional, methodical style of play, anchored by the dynamic Julius Erving and the talented playmaker Maurice Cheeks. The Lakers, on the other hand, adopted a relaxed, run-and-gun style that perfectly captured the essence of Los Angeles.

Riley had developed a new style of basketball, which was showcased in the Finals. Magic Johnson replaced the injured Kareem Abdul-Jabbar in Game 6, which made it very memorable. Magic, who was only 20 at the time, played center in a crucial match that would decide the winner. His versatility was shown as he recorded an incredible 42 points, 15 rebounds, and 7 assists while adjusting to the position with ease. The Lakers won 123-107, launching the Showtime era and winning their first title in eight years.

After winning the title, the Lakers became a dominant force in the NBA. The team's status as a consistent competitor was cemented in the ensuing years, marked by thrilling games and an entertaining style of basketball. In addition to winning titles, the Showtime Lakers expanded the definition of professional basketball and drew supporters from all backgrounds.

Along with their exciting style of play, the Lakers developed a distinct persona both on and off the court. The players embraced the celebrity lifestyle that came with their success, and the team came to represent the gloss and glamor of Los Angeles. Magic Johnson became well-known due to his remarkable talent and pleasant demeanor. The excitement in the arena was electrifying as the Lakers performed for crowded crowds, driven by the expectation of seeing something exceptional each time they took the floor.

The NBA is intricately entwined with the legacy of the Showtime era. It served as motivation for upcoming generations of coaches and athletes by highlighting the need for cooperation, ingenuity, and flexibility in response to the changing demands of the game. Riley's focus on mental toughness and conditioning became a defining characteristic of winning teams in the years that followed. Additionally, the NBA gained prominence throughout this time, attracting new followers and raising the sport's profile globally.

CHAPTER 3: THE ART OF WINNING

Riley's unique coaching style, motivational techniques, and his philosophy on building winning teams

Grasp Pat Riley's success in the NBA, especially during his tenure with the Miami Heat and Los Angeles Lakers, requires a grasp of his coaching philosophy and style. Riley, who is well-known for inspiring and motivating others, turned his teams into championship challengers by fostering a culture of excellence, discipline, and relentless will to win. His distinct style of teaching blended emotional intelligence with tactical knowledge to establish a personal connection with players and create an atmosphere where success became more than simply a goal—it became a way of life.

The Art of Winning

Riley's coaching style is based on the idea that winning is an art form that calls for a careful balancing act between skill, teamwork, and perseverance. He realized that while individual skill is important, a team's capacity to function as a unit is the real indicator of success. His personal experiences as a player, when he discovered the importance of teamwork and sacrifice on the court, served as the foundation for this comprehension.

Riley stressed that success necessitates a resilient and determined mindset in addition to skill. He frequently emphasized the value of mental toughness and convinced his athletes that they could conquer any challenge. This idea proved particularly pertinent during difficult games or season occasions. Riley used a variety of motivational strategies to ensure that his players remained focused and mentally prepared since he believed that the mental side of the game was equally as significant as the physical.

Motivational Techniques

Riley's use of vivid imagery and storytelling was one of his signature motivational strategies. His ability to depict achievement in a way that his players could relate to was exceptional. He encouraged his staff to see their potential by sharing success stories from his own and others' experiences. This strategy not only increased their drive but also assisted in forging a sense of unity among the players.

He was also a strong proponent of positive reinforcement. He frequently acknowledged and celebrated his teammates' achievements, no matter how minor. This exercise inspired players to take chances and challenge themselves, which promoted confidence and a sense of belonging. Riley fostered an atmosphere where players felt appreciated and inspired to strive for excellence by openly praising their diligence and commitment.

Riley was also renowned for his meticulous attention to detail. He carefully researched opponents and created customized game plans that capitalized on his team's advantages while highlighting their disadvantages. His focus on detail ensured that players were psychologically and physically ready to handle any situation that came up during games. Riley frequently conducted rigorous film sessions, breaking down plays and tactics to ensure players were aware of their roles. This dedication to planning strengthened the notion that hard effort and diligence were the keys to success.

Building Winning Teams

Riley's approach to creating successful teams was based on the ideas of chemistry and teamwork. He realized that relationships formed off the court were the key to success on it. He actively encouraged players to support one another on a personal and professional level by fostering a family-like environment within his teams.

This emphasis on unity was essential to creating a culture where players could flourish on their own while also contributing to the team's overall success.

He made it a point to know his players outside of their basketball skills in order to accomplish this. He made the effort to learn about their histories, driving forces, and individual challenges. Because of this relationship, he was able to modify his strategy to suit each player's unique requirements, which promoted loyalty and trust. For instance, he established a mentorship program with the Miami Heat where seasoned players assisted their less experienced teammates, furthering the concept of team development.

Riley also highlighted the value of physical training, arguing that a squad with strong conditioning could stay competitive over the demanding NBA season. He instituted rigorous training programs that frequently included accountability and discipline components similar to those seen in military training. In addition to enhancing players' performance, this dedication to fitness ingrained a discipline that influenced every facet of the organization.

Legacy of Winning

Riley's coaching philosophy and style came together to create an outstanding legacy that included numerous championships and a long-lasting effect on the teams he coached. Four NBA titles during his time with the Lakers in the 1980s cemented the team's dynastic reputation. With the Miami Heat, he carried on this success by assembling a championship team with players like Shaquille O'Neal and Dwyane Wade. Later, he added LeBron James and Chris Bosh to form a force that was renowned for its tenacity and resolve.

His method had a significant impact on basketball as a whole and on coaches who came after him. His values of careful preparation, mental toughness, and teamwork have become pillars of coaching philosophy throughout the league. Riley's teaching method has a wide-ranging impact, as seen by the fact that many modern coaches point to him as a mentor in their careers.

Pat Riley is a prime example of the art of winning, which goes beyond the specifics of basketball strategy. It includes a comprehensive strategy that emphasizes mental toughness, team dynamics, and interpersonal relationships. Riley made a lasting impression on the NBA and its future generations by redefining what it means to be a great coach in the league with his creative methods and dedication to creating teams that can win championships. His impact on players, teams, and the game of basketball itself is what truly defines his legacy, not just his wins and defeats.

CHAPTER 4: A NEW CHALLENGE – THE NEW YORK KNICKS

How Riley transformed the Knicks into contenders and embraced a tougher, defensive style

When Pat Riley took over as head coach of the New York Knicks in the middle of the 1990s, it was a turning point in the team's history because he wanted to turn around a faltering squad and change its image. Riley faced the difficult task of turning the Knicks into serious contenders following his storied career with the Los Angeles Lakers when he made a name for himself as one of the NBA's top coaches. What followed was an incredible adventure that not only changed the team's style of play but also infused New York basketball with a ferocious spirit of competition.

The Knicks were in ruins when Riley took over as manager in 1991. Despite its legendary past, the team had just finished a string of poor seasons and had yet to take home an NBA title since 1973. The Knicks needed help playing consistently and needed a clear sense of who they were. Riley was the individual to bring about the obvious cultural change that was required. Riley recognised that adjusting to the qualities of his existing team would be essential in this new setting, drawing on his prior experiences with the Showtime Lakers, where a fast-paced offence was paramount.

Riley turned his attention to defense after realizing that the Knicks lacked the Lakers' offensive potency. His concept was based on the idea that tenacity, determination, and superior defensive play are what win championships. Early in the 1990s, the NBA was changing, with clubs emphasizing defensive tactics to offset high-scoring offenses. Riley envisioned a club in

New York that would be rugged and resilient, traits that appealed to the city's fervent supporters.

His overhaul of the Knicks started with a focus on discipline and physical training. He implemented strict training plans intended to improve the players' fitness and ensure they were ready to play his demanding style. His first goal was to challenge his players to adopt a work ethic that would set the standard for the entire organization by fostering a sense of dedication and accountability.

Centre Patrick Ewing, the team's spokesperson and a gifted player whose potential had yet to be reached, played a significant role in this change. Riley understood that maximizing Ewing's potential would be essential to the Knicks' success after he had endured years of postseason disappointments. Riley helped Ewing develop into a more forceful leader both on and off the court by using motivational approaches and one-on-one coaching sessions. In response, Ewing became a defensive anchor for the club and started playing more aggressively.

Riley also gave top priority to hiring athletes who shared his values of grit and tenacity. He brought in athletes noted for their aggressiveness and perseverance, such as Anthony Mason and Charles Oakley. Former All-Star Oakley gave the Knicks a tough presence in the frontcourt, and Mason's adaptability and defensive skills were a wonderful match for Ewing. In addition to improving the team's defensive ability, these players helped to cultivate a work ethic and commitment.

He started to emphasize defense as the 1992–1993 season drew near. In stark contrast to the high-octane offense he had previously designed in Los Angeles, the Knicks adopted a gritty, hard-nosed style of play. Riley's defensive philosophy was based on the ideas of intensity, rotation, and communication. He gave his players a sense of urgency by stressing the value of playing aggressive defense and putting opponents in awkward positions.

The Knicks' stifling defense gained them notoriety right away. Riley emphasized the value of defensive rebounding to secure possessions and urged his team to exert constant pressure both on and off the ball. Thanks to their defensive perseverance, the Knicks were able to contend with the top teams in the NBA, which laid the groundwork for their success. Riley used tactics that frequently involved full-court pressure, making opponents respond to the Knicks' intensity right away.

The Knicks concluded the 1993 season with the league's top defensive rating, demonstrating the team's defensive dominance. Their ability to impede opposition offenses became a distinguishing characteristic of their identity, as they gave up the fewest points per game. Riley's dedication to defense made the Knicks one of the NBA's most formidable teams, gaining them notoriety and admiration across the league.

Riley's impact went beyond tactical modifications; he also highlighted the value of resilience and mental toughness. He realized that having a mindset that could overcome hardship was just as important for playoff success as having physical prowess. He taught his athletes this mindset, encouraging them to rise to challenges and see failures as chances for personal development.

The 1994 NBA Playoffs were one of the pivotal times in the Knicks' metamorphosis. After ending the regular season with a solid record, the Knicks went into the postseason with confidence. When they played the fierce Chicago Bulls in the Eastern Conference playoffs, their grit and resolve were put to the test. The Bulls, led by Michael Jordan, were considered the team to defeat and had been the defending champions.

The Knicks' development under Riley's leadership was demonstrated throughout the series. They made a lasting impact with their tenacity and defensive effort throughout a thrilling seven-game duel. The Knicks won the crucial Game 5 after a fierce battle that perfectly captured their new identity. A pivotal moment in the

Knicks' journey occurred when they overcame a series deficit to win the pivotal Game 7.

For the first time since the early 1970s, the Knicks made it to the NBA Finals after continuing their postseason success. The Knicks showed their tenacity against the Houston Rockets by persevering through difficult games and adjusting to their rivals' difficulties. Even though they lost in the Finals, the experience proved the value of Riley's coaching style and cemented their place as contenders.

Riley's time with the Knicks not only made the team a serious contender but also had a lasting impact on both the team and the city of New York. Reflecting the city itself, the franchise adopted a new brand based on toughness and tenacity. Riley's focus on mental toughness and defense became ingrained in the Knicks' basketball culture, impacting players and coaches in subsequent generations.

His teaching technique affected the community and spectators in addition to the players on the floor. The Knicks' ardent supporters were won over by their dedication to perseverance and hard work, and they valued the team's fortitude and resolve. With supporters uniting behind a squad that embodied the spirit of the city, Madison Square Garden turned into a stronghold of support.

Riley's impact on the Knicks' basketball philosophy persisted even after he left the team in 1995. The team adopted his defensive mentality as a defining characteristic, and the knowledge he gained during his time there prepared the way for further achievements. In an effort to maintain the tradition Riley had started, the Knicks would keep emphasizing toughness and physicality.

CHAPTER 5: MIAMI HEAT – MORE THAN JUST A COACH

Riley's transition to the Miami Heat, from head coach to team president, and his vision for the franchise

A pivotal period in Pat Riley's career and the development of the team was his move to the Miami Heat. Riley started a new adventure that would change his legacy in the NBA after a legendary time with the New York Knicks when he became one of the most successful coaches in NBA history. The Miami Heat, a young team, has seen highs and lows since its founding in 1988. Under Riley's leadership, the team not only changed on the court but also developed a unique character that connected with Miami's community and supporters.

Riley made the calculated choice to leave the turbulent world of New York basketball behind when he moved to Miami in 1995. Riley was seeking a new beginning after his time with the Knicks ended bitterly, as he resigned after a poor playoff elimination. There was an interesting chance with the Miami Heat. Despite having a solid squad at the time, the team needed help staying consistent and determining its course. Riley was viewed as the impetus required to unleash the team's potential because of his championship background and unparalleled coaching expertise.

He took charge and got to work right away. There was a noticeable sense of urgency to improve the Heat's record since they had just ended a season with a 32-50 record. Riley had faith in the team's undeveloped talent, which included Tim Hardaway and Alonzo Mourning. He also saw potential in the supporters, who were ready for a successful team to liven up South Florida. In order to realize his goal, Riley made it apparent that he wanted to establish a culture of competition that valued diligence, self-control, and—above all—winning.

Riley instituted a strict training schedule as one of his first actions as head coach. He was well-known for his rigorous teaching methods and dedication to fitness, emphasizing the value of preparation and conditioning. He believed that performance on the court was closely tied to one's level of physical preparedness. In addition, he tried to develop a strong defensive identity, which he had developed while playing with the Knicks. Riley recognized that a team needed to be a defensive powerhouse in order to compete in the NBA at a high level.

He saw Alonzo Mourning's potential as the foundation of his new vision. Two-time All-Star Mourning was renowned for his ability to block shots and his intense competitive spirit. He would become the face of the squad and a representation of its newfound emphasis on toughness under Riley's tutelage. Riley wanted Mourning to set the example for the rest of the team and taught him the value of leadership. Mourning's game improved as a result of the coach's influence, and he had a career year in 1999 with averages of 21.6 points, 10.4 rebounds, and 3.9 blocks per game.

Riley was aware that it was essential to surround his star player with the appropriate supporting cast in addition to Mourning. By making savvy roster moves, he acquired players who matched his idea for a tough, competitive club. Point guard Tim Hardaway, who contributed speed, skill, and experience to the backcourt, was one of the team's most important acquisitions. Together, Mourning and Hardaway formed a strong team that would support the franchise for many years to come.

Under Riley's direction, the Heat started to show improvement as the new century drew near. The 1999–2000 season saw the team qualify for the playoffs for the first time since 1997 at the latest. Even though the Heat lost to the New York Knicks in the opening round, it was a priceless experience. Riley's emphasis on creating a culture of competition was beginning to bear fruit, and the squad was progressively becoming more respected throughout the league.

Riley's career path underwent a dramatic change as a result of his success as Miami's head coach. In 2001, after leading the Heat to a franchise-best 50-win season, he decided to leave coaching and take on the position of team president. As a result of this change, he was able to concentrate on the more general facets of franchise development, such as player acquisitions, team strategy, and the organization's overall orientation.

His goals for the Miami Heat as team president went beyond winning games. His goal was to establish a business that exemplified the virtues of perseverance, hard effort, and community involvement. He recognized that an all-encompassing strategy involving player development, marketing, and scouting was necessary for NBA success. Under his direction, the Heat started to establish a reputation as a destination for skilled athletes by offering competitive pay together with the appeal of Miami's lively culture.

One of Riley's most important achievements was his ability to spot and draw elite talent to Miami. His status as a winner and coach provided opportunities that many other teams were unable to access. The Heat's 2003 selection of Marquette University shooting guard Dwyane Wade was a game-changer for the team. Riley accepted Wade into a society that valued excellence after realizing his enormous potential. Riley's leadership style and Wade's explosive athleticism combined to create a team that might contend for a championship.

Riley also played a key role in putting together Wade's formidable supporting cast. O'Neal's arrival gave the Heat a powerful interior presence, and he and Wade became one of the most effective duos in NBA history. As the Heat emerged as a dominant force in the Eastern Conference, Riley's vision for the team began to take shape.

The Miami Heat achieved unprecedented success in the 2005–06 season, culminating in their first NBA title. Under Riley's direction, the group demonstrated a combination of skill, expertise, and tenacity. With a 52-30 record at the end of the regular season, the Heat had an incredible playoff run.

The Heat faced the reigning champion Detroit Pistons in the Eastern Conference Finals. In an arduous series, the Heat overcame a 2-0 deficit to win four games in a row and guarantee their spot in the NBA Finals. Throughout this difficult series, Riley's tactical adaptations, inspirational methods, and capacity to motivate his players were all on full display.

The Dallas Mavericks, who had already defeated the Heat in the 2006 NBA Finals, faced them in the Finals. The pressure was evident, and the stakes were bigger this time. Both sides traded victories in the hotly-contested series. But in the end, Riley's background and the Heat's tenacity won out. In the Finals, Dwyane Wade led the Heat to victory with an incredible effort, averaging 34.7 points per game.

Riley's reputation in the Miami Heat's history was cemented on June 20, 2006, when the team celebrated their first NBA title. The triumph was the result of years of arduous effort and sacrifice, and his vision, leadership, and drive to create a winning culture had paid off.

Following the championship win, Riley's responsibilities as team president changed. Negotiating the difficulties of the wage cap and roster management, he played a crucial role in keeping the Heat competitive. Thanks to his ability to spot talent and make important additions, the Heat maintained their status as a consistent postseason challenger throughout the 2000s.

Riley's goals went beyond short-term achievement; he wanted to create a winning culture that would last for many years. His focus on player development became a pillar of the franchise's strategy. To find up-and-coming talent, the Heat invested in scouting and analytics and implemented extensive training programs under his direction.

He kept changing his approach when the NBA started to change in the 2010s. Superteam creation and player movement became commonplace, which led Riley to adopt creative roster-building strategies. In a league that is always changing, his readiness to adapt to the game helped the Heat stay relevant and competitive.

Riley's efforts to assemble a winning squad paid off once more in 2010 when he enticed Chris Bosh and LeBron James to join Dwyane Wade in Miami. This historic decision began the "Big Three" era, which resulted in four straight trips to the NBA Finals and two additional titles in 2012 and 2013. In addition to transforming the Miami Heat, Riley's vision made the team a dominant force in the NBA.

CHAPTER 6: HEAT CULTURE – A LEGACY OF DISCIPLINE

Exploring the "Heat Culture" that Riley established, emphasizing discipline, resilience, and teamwork

Pat Riley's impact on the Miami Heat went beyond simple coaching techniques and game plans; he created the "Heat Culture," a concept that came to represent the team's identity. The team's success was built on this culture, which also shaped the players' personalities by emphasizing discipline, resiliency, and teamwork. Riley established a culture that not only won titles but also changed the lives of players, coaches, and the Miami community by fusing personal experiences, professional beliefs, and an uncompromising dedication to perfection.

His playing career helped shape his grasp of what it takes to create a winning basketball team, and his coaching career furthered this expertise. He was aware that having talent by itself would not ensure success; teams with a shared dedication to a common objective are the most successful. He realized he needed to establish discipline in the organization when he took over as head coach of the Miami Heat.

Riley started by creating strict training schedules that required athletes to give their all. In the NBA, where games are frequently decided in the closing minutes, he thought physical conditioning was essential for success. His focus on fitness became a defining feature of the Heat's training program, as players were frequently put through rigorous exercises meant to test their limits. Riley wanted all of his players to be in top physical shape and prepared to meet his exacting requirements when they arrived at training camp.

He believed that discipline involved more than just following training plans; it also involved embracing an attitude that placed a high value on accountability and responsibility. He urged players to assume responsibility for their positions on the team. This required students to hold themselves accountable for their performance, show up on time for practices, and give their all during games. Riley's motto was straightforward: "No excuses." As a result of the emphasis on discipline, players were expected to bring their best selves to the court every day.

Since Riley recognised that the path to success is sometimes paved with obstacles and disappointments, the idea of resilience became essential to the Heat Culture. True champions are distinguished not just by their triumphs but also by their capacity to overcome hardship. Based on his personal experiences as a coach and player, Riley gave his players the confidence that they could conquer any challenge.

During the 2006 NBA Finals, the Heat displayed one of their most remarkable moments of tenacity. After losing to the Dallas Mavericks 2-0, the Heat were under a lot of strain and scrutiny. In response, Riley emphasized to his team their resilience in the face of difficulty. He underlined the significance of maintaining composure, staying focused, and having faith in their group's talents. The squad responded really well to this message, and they came together to win four games in a row and win the title.

Riley aimed to foster a team mindset among his athletes because he believed that perseverance went beyond individual accomplishments. He urged people to help each other, especially during difficult times. During sessions, he would design competitive exercises that mimicked high-stress scenarios, teaching players how to react appropriately in high-stakes scenarios. This dedication to cultivating mental toughness was a key component of Heat Culture.

The most distinctive feature of Heat Culture was its emphasis on teamwork, even though discipline and perseverance were essential elements. Riley understood that basketball is essentially a team sport and that cooperation and teamwork are the only ways to succeed.

He aimed to establish an atmosphere in which players put the team's demands ahead of their own.

Riley's management style promoted candid dialogue and teamwork among the players. He believed that building trust on the court required cultivating solid connections in the locker room, so he planned team-building exercises outside of basketball to help with this. Riley also knew that strengthening relationships off the court would result in better chemistry during games, whether that was through group activities or volunteer work.

The Heat's formation of a "Big Three" with Chris Bosh, LeBron James, and Dwyane Wade during the 2010–2011 season was a notable example of this teamwork culture. LeBron James's arrival, in particular, created a special difficulty because it forced players to adjust to new roles and expectations. Riley's strategy placed a strong emphasis on selflessness; he urged each player to realize that their success as an individual was inextricably linked to the team's success.

Riley frequently reminded the players in the locker room that winning titles was more important than receiving individual honors. He made sure everyone felt heard and respected by facilitating conversations among the players to address any issues over roles or playing time. In addition to improving the "Big Three's" on-court play, this dedication to cooperation and teamwork set the stage for the Heat's two straight titles in 2012 and 2013.

His goals for Heat Culture went beyond the team's short-term success; they included leaving a legacy of excellence that would last for many generations. He held that shared beliefs and consistency over time create culture. Riley underlined the value of player development and mentoring to maintain Heat Culture. To promote a culture of development and learning, he wanted more experienced players to share their wisdom with their less experienced teammates.

Riley put in place a thorough player development program that includes leadership, nutrition, and mental toughness sessions in addition to skill training. He expanded the team's perspective on what it meant to be a professional athlete by inviting coaches, sports psychologists, and previous players to speak. The notion that success is not only determined by titles won but also by character and personal development was strengthened by this dedication to holistic development.

During the 2011–2012 season, when the club encountered a great deal of hardship, including injuries and lineup changes, the impact of Heat Culture was evident. But the values of self-control, perseverance, and cooperation never wavered. The players exemplified Heat Culture by supporting one another. They won an NBA championship and had a 66-win season because of their dedication to one another and their mutual faith in their abilities.

Pat Riley recognised that Heat Culture permeated the community in addition to the basketball court. In his opinion, the franchise needed to interact with both its supporters and the city of Miami if it was to succeed. The Heat launched a number of community service projects to support wellness, education, and youth sports. This dedication to giving back struck a chord with supporters and facilitated a closer bond between the community and the squad.

Riley has underlined the value of serving as a role model for Miami's young athletes. He thought it was the players' duty to motivate the following generation. The Heat players would tell their tales, talk about the importance of hard work, and inspire children to follow their aspirations through outreach initiatives and school visits. In addition to strengthening the team's standing as a community-focused organization, this strategy upheld the principles ingrained in Heat Culture.

Heat Culture kept developing over the years, according to the NBA's shifting conditions. Riley recognised that the franchise needed to embrace innovation and adaptability in order to sustain a winning culture. He stayed dedicated to applying the most recent developments in analytics, player development tactics, and sports science. The Heat gained a reputation for being progressive, frequently setting the standard in fields like injury prevention and recovery.

Under Riley's direction, the Heat adopted the values of inclusivity and diversity. He understood that a group of people with diverse backgrounds may provide a range of viewpoints and concepts. This diversity encouraged innovation and teamwork, strengthening Heat Culture's foundation even more.

CHAPTER 7: THE BIG THREE ERA

The formation of Miami's "Big Three" with LeBron James, Dwyane Wade, and Chris Bosh, and the pursuit of championships

The emergence of Miami's "Big Three" was a turning point in NBA history. It altered not only the Miami Heat franchise but also the professional basketball landscape as a whole. In the summer of 2010, LeBron James, Dwyane Wade, and Chris Bosh formed a partnership that would revolutionize player cooperation and significantly improve the Heat's standing as a title contender.

Long before the players formally teamed up, preparations were made for this historic event. Already well-liked in Miami, Dwyane Wade had become one of the best shooting guards in the game. He became a pillar of the Heat after his spectacular performance in the 2006 NBA Finals, where he guided the team to their first title. However, the team found it difficult to sustain steady success following Wade's push for the championship. Wade and the Heat's management started talking about the prospect of bringing in other superstar players to supplement Wade's abilities after realizing the team needed reinforcements.

LeBron James, who had played for the Cleveland Cavaliers for the first seven years of his career, was also under growing criticism for failing to win an NBA championship. Even though LeBron had already won two MVP awards by 2010, he still felt the need to win despite his enormous success as an individual. Because of their friendships and common goals, rumors that LeBron would like to join Wade in Miami intensified in the run-up to free agency. LeBron had had trouble finding the perfect supporting cast in Cleveland, and Miami's appeal—both the city and its basketball culture—started to solidify as a strong contender.

Another player at a turning point in his career was Chris Bosh, who was a standout power forward for the Toronto Raptors at the time. Bosh had made a name for himself as one of the league's most adaptable big players, renowned for both his defensive and scoring skills. Like LeBron, though, he had not yet felt the rush of winning a title. Bosh started thinking about his future and what it would take to reach his ultimate aim as the free agency season drew near. Bosh's thoughts of teaming up with Wade and LeBron started to solidify, particularly following a crucial exchange with Wade at the 2010 All-Star Game in Dallas, where the two players talked about the prospect of playing together.

NBA fans and commentators were holding their breath as July 1, 2010, drew near, ready to see what would happen during the free agency period. In a crucial meeting in Miami, LeBron, Wade, and Bosh talked about their common goal of success. They understood that creating a super squad would necessitate sacrifice, with each player possibly sacrificing their stats and recognition in favor of the team's overall success. The conventional NBA approach, in which elite players usually fought for supremacy, was drastically different from this.

LeBron made his choice to join the Miami Heat public on July 8, 2010, in a televised special called "The Decision." Many were taken aback by his decision, both because of the drama that surrounded the incident and because of the ramifications it held for the NBA's future. Wade and Bosh soon did the same, completing the "Big Three" and making the Heat immediate contenders for the championship. There was a lot of enthusiasm surrounding the trio's arrival in Miami, but there was also a lot of criticism. A contentious discussion concerning the league's shifting dynamics resulted from numerous fans and analysts questioning the morality of players banding together to succeed.

The Heat's expectations skyrocketed after the "Big Three" were added. In addition to serving as the team's president, Pat Riley, the creator of this cohesive unit, was crucial in coordinating the shift to a championship culture. In addition to adding supporting players who may enhance their playing style, he underlined the significance of developing synergy amongst the three stars. Important players like Shane Battier, Mario Chalmers, and Udonis Haslem strengthened the Heat's squad by providing the tenacity and resolve required for a championship run.

The basketball community was enthralled with the Heat's potential as the 2010–2011 season got underway. They had to overcome the tremendous expectations put on them and integrate three dominating personalities into a cohesive team, among other urgent problems. After a difficult beginning marked by a string of defeats and criticism from both fans and the media, the "Big Three" persisted and eventually found their rhythm. With a 58-24 record at the end of the season, they had moments of genius that suggested the greatness they would eventually achieve.

There were several high points throughout the Heat's 2011 playoff run. They faced the Boston Celtics, a seasoned squad that had previously thwarted the Heat's hopes of making the playoffs after defeating the Philadelphia 76ers in the first round. The series was a demanding seven-game contest that demonstrated the team's development as they overcame hardship to win. For the first time as a team, the Heat made it to the NBA Finals, where they faced the Dallas Mavericks, who were vying for their first title.

The NBA Finals in 2011 turned out to be a turning point for the "Big Three." Their capacity to produce under pressure was called into doubt after they lost the first two games of the series. The Heat, on the other hand, bounced back and won Game 3 spectacularly. However, the narrative would eventually reveal the trio's weaknesses. The Heat led the series, but they made mistakes at pivotal points that let the Mavericks pull off a historic comeback and win the title in six games. For the "Big Three," this defeat served as a painful reminder of the value of cooperation and mental toughness in high-pressure scenarios.

The disappointment of the 2011 Finals strengthened the Heat's resolve to win in the upcoming seasons. Riley and the group changed their emphasis, focussing on the importance of better camaraderie, mental toughness, and dedication to defense. The trio promised to return stronger after reflecting on their combined performance and accepting personal responsibility for their parts in the defeat.

The Heat returned to form in the 2011–2012 campaign. Riley's focus on defense started to pay off, and they adopted an unrelenting work ethic. The Heat finished the regular season with a franchise-record 66 wins because of a mix of their aggressive offense and resilient defence. Because of their unselfish ball movement and fast-paced style of play, the three became one of the league's most feared teams, always destroying opponents.

The playoffs were a test for the "Big Three." They used a combination of skill, strategy, and willpower to defeat the Boston Celtics, Indiana Pacers, and New York Knicks. The Oklahoma City Thunder, led by James Harden, Russell Westbrook, and a youthful Kevin Durant, defeated the Heat in the NBA Finals. The Heat's skill and experience won out, and they won their second title, creating a lasting legacy for the "Big Three."

The Heat aimed to defend their title and cement their legacy the next season. Unprecedented success characterized the 2012–2013 season, which ended with a franchise-high 66 victories. The team also demonstrated their dominance and unity by going on an incredible 27-game winning run. They overcame obstacles and showed tenacity in the playoffs, defeating the Indiana Pacers, Chicago Bulls, and Milwaukee Bucks to advance to the Finals once more.

The San Antonio Spurs, a club renowned for their strategic skill and disciplined play, played the Heat in the 2013 NBA Finals. The series was a demanding seven-game contest with several high-stakes moments. The Heat won back-to-back titles after overcoming a 3-2 series deficit to win the championship spectacularly. As evidence of their dedication to one another and the sacrifices they made for the sake of society, LeBron, Wade, and Bosh shared in the celebration.

The Miami "Big Three" period changed how clubs built championship lineups, leaving a lasting impression on the NBA. In addition to their incredible success together, LeBron, Wade, and Bosh inspired upcoming generations of athletes to work together and pursue titles as a team. Their history of excellence, perseverance, and teamwork still influences and shapes basketball today.

CHAPTER 8: LEADERSHIP BEYOND THE COURT

Riley's impact as a mentor, team builder, and innovator within the NBA

Beyond his outstanding achievements as a player and coach, Pat Riley has had a significant impact on the NBA as a representation of innovative professional basketball leadership, mentoring, and teamwork. Riley has shown a deep comprehension of the intricacies of individual player development, the dynamics of teamwork, and the significance of culture throughout his career. In addition to the accomplishments of the teams he has coached, his leadership influence can be seen in the lives of many business people and athletes he has guided.

Riley's leadership approach stems from a thorough comprehension of the psychological elements of both the game and the participants. According to him, a coach's job is not just to plan and lead from the sidelines; it's also to be an inspiration to players, inspiring them to realize their greatest potential. This viewpoint is mirrored in his method of player mentorship, which combines unflinching support with harsh love. He has continuously underlined the value of self-control, responsibility, and diligence, fostering an atmosphere where players feel both challenged and empowered.

His ability to build solid team cultures is among his most noteworthy leadership accomplishments. Starting with the Los Angeles Lakers, where he helped create the "Showtime" era and continuing through his revolutionary work with the Miami Heat, Riley has always placed a high value on creating a winning culture that encourages cooperation, resiliency, and common objectives. He realized that relationships made in the locker room are just as important to success as skill on the court. Riley has built teams that rely on the combined strength of his players rather than just their talents by emphasizing communication, teamwork, and respect for one another.

Riley's mentoring of some of the best players in the game is arguably the strongest example of his impact on his teammates. Early on, he realized that optimizing his players' performance required an awareness of their distinct personalities and motives. During his tenure with the Lakers, for instance, he became close with Magic Johnson, who not only became an important player but also exemplified Riley's teaching style. Johnson thrived as a player and a leader on the floor because Riley knew how to capitalize on his energy and charisma. Riley's method was characterized by his ability to relate to players personally, which set an example for other coaches to follow.

He had to start from scratch in order to create a competitive squad when he joined the Miami Heat. Riley's vision and leadership helped the Heat become one of the league's most respected teams, even though they were thought of as a weak franchise at first. He realized that creating a winning culture required more than simply hiring talented people; it also required a dedication to the principles of perseverance, hard effort, and sacrifice. Riley underlined the significance of forging an identity based on cooperation and defense, ideas that would come to represent the Heat brand.

Riley's creative leadership style is demonstrated by the "Heat Culture" he created. This culture is distinguished by its focus on professionalism, discipline, and the unwavering pursuit of perfection. Riley's concept applies to everyone connected to the team, including the front office, coaches, and staff, in addition to the players on the floor. Riley has made sure that each member of the Heat family is aware of their part in the team's success by establishing these ideals throughout the entire organization.

He has been a trailblazer in player development as well. He has led the charge in acknowledging the value of holistic training methods, stressing both mental and physical preparation. Because he thought that a player's thinking could often determine the outcome of a game, he pioneered techniques that prioritized mental toughness. Riley established a new benchmark for how organizations approached player development by collaborating closely with sports psychologists and creating initiatives that promote mental toughness. The NBA has been impacted for a long time by this progressive mindset, which has shaped how coaches and organizations prioritize performance psychology and mental wellness.

Riley's impact as a mentor goes beyond the athletes he has trained. Numerous previous players and helpers of his have achieved success in coaching and management. Examples of Riley's mentoring impact include Erik Spoelstra, who was originally his assistant coach and is currently the head coach of the Miami Heat. Spoelstra frequently talks about the priceless lessons he learnt from Riley, such as the value of planning ahead, being flexible, and building relationships with players. This mentoring legacy has produced a generation of leaders who uphold the principles Riley taught them. Influence is also seen in the way he has handled the NBA's changing environment. He stands out as an innovator because of his readiness to adjust and welcome change. By using cutting-edge data, utilizing player mobility, or investigating novel coaching theories, he has continuously defied accepted wisdom. Throughout his tenure, his ability to predict trends and adjust to the league's shifting dynamics has kept him recognised and relevant.

His willingness to take chances and make audacious choices is another quality that distinguishes his leadership. An excellent illustration of his forward-thinking attitude is his pursuit of the "Big Three" in Miami. He wanted to change the NBA's landscape in addition to building a title contender when he brought together LeBron James, Dwyane Wade, and Chris Bosh. Although this choice was greeted with doubt and criticism, Riley stuck to his plan because he thought that these three superstars working together would result in long-term success. His capacity to accept danger while upholding a distinct goal of achievement is a prime example of what makes a great leader.

Riley's influence on the NBA also extends to his work as an author and motivational speaker. His book, "The Winner Within," offers a glimpse into his views on achievement, teamwork, and leadership. He has inspired athletes and people in other sectors to embrace the values of diligence, resiliency, and perseverance by sharing his experiences and advice with a wider audience through his writing and speaking engagements.

CHAPTER 9: THE RILEY PLAYBOOK – LESSONS IN SUCCESS AND RESILIENCE

Life lessons and core principles from Riley's playbook on leadership and success

A name often associated with basketball success, Pat Riley has built a legacy that goes well beyond the court. In addition to championship rings and honors, his path as a player, coach, and executive is replete with priceless lessons and fundamental ideas that have influenced his outlook on resilience and leadership. The "Riley Playbook," as it has become known, is a compilation of lessons learnt from his experiences that provide a road map for success in both life and sports.

Riley's concept is based on the steadfast confidence in the power of preparation. He has made it clear throughout his career that hard work and an unwavering dedication to excellence are the keys to success rather than chance or luck. Riley has always argued for careful planning, whether it is for a pivotal game or the upcoming season. His famous quote, "Success is where preparation meets opportunity," perfectly captures his philosophy. Riley believes that every little detail counts, from analyzing the patterns of opponents to making sure that players are prepared both psychologically and physically for the challenges that lie ahead. Teams are able to successfully carry out their game plans because of this careful planning, which gives players confidence and fosters an accountable culture.

Another crucial lesson from the Riley Playbook is the value of flexibility in addition to preparation. Professional sports are continually changing, and Riley has always understood how important it is to modify tactics to overcome new obstacles. His career demonstrates this ideaHis career demonstrates this idea, as he has effectively switched from the fast-paced "Showtime" Lakers of the 1980s to the gritty defensive approach that defined his tenure with the New York Knicks. His capacity to adapt and welcome change stems from a deep awareness that success can be hampered by rigidity. Riley teaches that adaptability and flexibility are critical for long-term success in a world where things might change suddenly.

Riley also emphasizes the value of relationships and team chemistry in his leadership style. He understands that a united team frequently performs better than a group of disparate skills. He has placed a high value on developing close bonds with his players throughout his coaching career in order to create an atmosphere of mutual respect and trust. He has frequently said, "You can't lead without loving your players," highlighting the fact that true concern for the people you are leading is the foundation of great leadership. Riley fosters a sense of loyalty and belonging among his players by fostering these ties, which in turn strengthens their will to achieve as a team.

The Riley Playbook also emphasizes the importance of resilience in the face of hardship. Riley has faced many difficulties along the way, including difficult defeats in championship series and figuring out the intricacies of team dynamics. He has continuously shown that obstacles are chances for improvement rather than failures. He frequently discusses the value of recovering from setbacks, reminding athletes that real champions are determined by how they handle setbacks rather than by their capacity to prevent them. Riley teaches his athletes that resilience is a skill that can be acquired with tenacity, willpower, and an optimistic outlook. This idea is particularly pertinent in a cutthroat setting like the NBA, where a team's ability to bounce back from setbacks frequently determines its level of success.

The importance of accountability is also emphasized in the Riley Playbook. Riley thinks that everyone on the team needs to be accountable for their respective roles and duties. Accountability is a complex idea that includes both keeping oneself accountable for one's performance and motivating others to do the same. Riley has frequently established a climate of mutual respect and high expectations, giving players the confidence to hold one another to a high standard. Members of the team form bonds as a result of this accountability, which increases their motivation to achieve as a group.

Riley was renowned for his intense intensity and burning passion during his coaching tenure. Passion is infectious and essential for motivating people. His well-known "Riley Rules" were:
A series of guidelines that described his expectations for players.
Stressing the value of diligence.
Self-control.
Dedication to the team's success.
This zeal and a clear idea of success inspired players to give it their all on the court. Riley inspires the team to aim for excellence by bringing a feeling of purpose to the group through his passionate leadership style.

Riley's playbook also emphasizes the importance of having a good work ethic. He has continuously promoted the notion that hard work is the primary differentiator for success rather than skill alone. Riley's career serves as an example of this dedication; both as a player and subsequently, as a coach, he was renowned for his unwavering work ethic. He highlights that excellence is the product of constant work and devotion rather than an accident. This work ethic is instilled in his teams through intense preparation, practice, and training, making sure that players know how important it is to put in the effort every single day.

Riley's worldview emphasizes the value of vision as well. He is adamant that effective leaders need to have a clear idea of what they hope to accomplish. The team is guided by this vision, which gives them direction and a sense of purpose. Riley has consistently communicated his objectives in a way that his players can understand, which helps them see the wider picture. He has continuously pushed his staff to have large dreams and high expectations, reaffirming the notion that genuine success frequently results from setting and achieving great goals.

Furthermore, a key component of Riley's playbook is his emphasis on lifelong learning and self-improvement. He understands that the most effective leaders are those who are dedicated to their personal development. He has always looked for ways to learn from others, whether it is by reading, receiving mentoring, or interacting with other coaches and athletes. His dedication to ongoing development not only strengthens his leadership abilities but also serves as a model for his teammates. According to Riley, the quest for knowledge and self-improvement is a lifetime endeavor, and people who embrace it are better able to handle life's obstacles.

Last but not least, believing in the strength of an optimistic outlook is among the Riley Playbook's most important lessons. Riley is aware that attitude plays a big role in both life and sports success. He advocates the notion that performance can be greatly impacted by keeping a cheerful attitude despite hardship. Riley assists his players in overcoming obstacles and maintaining focus on their objectives by cultivating a culture that promotes positivity and perseverance. Players feel supported and inspired to take chances in this upbeat atmosphere, which eventually results in more success.

CHAPTER 10: THE LASTING LEGACY OF PAT RILEY

How Riley's impact is still felt across the league and his enduring influence on the sport

Pat Riley has impacted the NBA in ways that go beyond time, location, and specific teams. His impact is deeply ingrained in the league, influencing its tactics, ethos, and even the composition of clubs. Riley has made a lasting impact on basketball that is still felt strongly in the game today, starting with his early playing days and continuing through his remarkable coaching career and executive position.

His impact is especially noticeable in the way coaching philosophies have changed in the NBA. He started the fast-paced, high-scoring "Showtime" offense while still a novice coach with the Los Angeles Lakers. This was a cultural shift that prioritized flare, excitement, and entertainment, and it wasn't just about the Xs and Os. This strategy changed how teams played the game and produced players like Magic Johnson, Kareem Abdul-Jabbar, and James Worthy. In the present day, the league's current trend towards faster play and higher scoring has traces of such a "Showtime" mentality. Fast breaks, three-point shooting, and an emphasis on offensive efficiency—all characteristics of Riley's creative style—are given priority by teams.

Riley's impact also goes beyond style; it affects the very mindset that teams function with. He was a trailblazer in highlighting the psychological elements of the game and mental toughness. He popularized the notion that mental toughness is just as important to winning as physical prowess during his time with the Lakers. His strategies, which included motivational speeches and visualization exercises, encouraged players to persevere through hardship and perform well under duress. As a result of Riley's early recognition of the value of psychological readiness in high-stakes scenarios, mental conditioning is now a common element of NBA training programs.

Many modern NBA coaches have their coaching views firmly rooted in Riley's ideas of team building and leadership. His focus on building a solid team culture, encouraging responsibility, and keeping lines of communication open has turned into a model for league success. These ideas have been embraced and modified by coaches such as Erik Spoelstra, who trained under Riley while working for the Miami Heat. Spoelstra demonstrated how Riley's ideas could be successfully applied to build a championship-caliber squad during the Heat's "Big Three" period, which featured LeBron James, Dwyane Wade, and Chris Bosh. Riley's lasting influence is reflected in the Heat's culture of sacrifice, discipline, and resiliency.

Riley's influence can also be seen in the way teams handle scouting and player development. Building from within is crucial, and he has been a steadfast supporter of the idea that a great team must put its players' development first. With several teams making significant investments in their player development programs and nurturing young talent through their farm systems, this idea has gained support throughout the league. Since teams have realized that long-term success is frequently based on a foundation of homegrown players who exemplify the team's ideals and culture, Riley's effect is evident in the attention placed on developing a pipeline of talent.

Teams' perceptions of their front offices and executive positions have changed as a result of Riley's contributions to the league. He has proven the need to have leaders who have a thorough understanding of both coaching and management as a successful coach who transitioned into an executive role. Because of his dual viewpoint, he is able to make well-informed decisions that take into account the team's long-term goals in addition to its immediate demands. This strategy has motivated a new generation of executives who place a high value on management and coaching, working together to make sure that every choice is in keeping with the franchise's overall objectives.

Pat Riley's legacy extends beyond his accomplishments; it is also evident in the accomplishments of innumerable athletes and coaches who he has impacted. Many NBA greats have benefited greatly from his mentoring, which has shaped their careers by giving them the direction, insight, and resources they need to succeed on and off the court. Players like LeBron James and Dwyane Wade have frequently mentioned Riley as a key influence in their careers, attributing to him the value of perseverance, hard effort, and a never-ending quest for greatness. Riley's lessons and philosophies are being passed down through generations of players and coaches, ensuring that his influence will continue to reverberate across the league.

Riley is dedicated to winning not only on the court but throughout the entire organisation. He has always promoted a comprehensive strategy for franchise development, understanding that teamwork is essential to success. His commitment to fostering an atmosphere where all members of the team—coaches, players, and staff—feel appreciated and invested in the team's success has established a benchmark that many teams aim to meet. In today's NBA, where cooperation and chemistry are crucial for success, this emphasis on unity and collaboration has grown in significance.

He has had a major role in forming the NBA's business side in addition to his efforts on the court. His proficiency in handling the intricacies of media relations, player contracts, and club operations has established a standard for league executives. He is aware of the significance of developing a strong fan base and brand, both of which are becoming more and more important in today's sports environment. Riley's astute business sense has shaped how teams interact with their communities and promote themselves, guaranteeing that the NBA will continue to be a prosperous industry both on and off the court.

Riley's ideas and methods are still applicable as the league develops. His impact is evident in the tactics used by winning teams, the culture they cultivate, and the focus placed on players' mental and emotional health. The values Riley promoted during his career are echoed by many clubs today, which place a heavy focus on accountability, flexibility, preparation, and a strong work ethic.

CONCLUSION

A Game Visionary

As we come to the end of this examination of Pat Riley's remarkable life and career, it is evident that he is more than just a coach or businessman; he is a visionary who has influenced basketball in ways that are still relevant today. Riley has had a significant and varied influence on the NBA from his early playing days to his time as a coach and executive, leaving a legacy that goes well beyond the titles and honors he has amassed.

Riley's path started on the court, where his unwavering determination and passion for competition shaped his subsequent pursuits. He gained a deep understanding of the game while playing for the San Diego Rockets and then the Los Angeles Lakers. This expertise extended beyond strategy to include leadership and teamwork dynamics. These formative early encounters taught him the value of teamwork, self-control, and perseverance—skills that would characterize his teaching philosophy and impact many athletes and coaches.

Riley, who went from being a player to a coach, changed the NBA's playing style with his creative approach. Basketball as a spectacle was redefined during the Lakers' "Showtime" era, which was more than just quick breaks and huge scores. Riley's deep knowledge of the game and its players was demonstrated by his ability to combine skill and strategy to create a winning atmosphere. His achievements during this period established the foundation for contemporary basketball and showed how a coach's vision might lead a team to success.

His impact increased even further after he joined the Miami Heat and then the New York Knicks. With the Knicks, he adopted a defensive style of play that revolutionized team relationships and showed that grit and tenacity could be just as successful as offensive skill.

His move to the Heat, where he served as team president in addition to being a coach, demonstrated his adaptability and astute business sense. He skilfully handled the intricacies of player development and roster construction, which led to the creation of the Miami "Big Three." In addition to bringing championships to Miami, this calculated maneuver established a standard for how teams should use star power to their advantage.

One of Riley's greatest contributions to basketball is his emphasis on culture, which has come to be known as "Heat Culture." This idea fosters an atmosphere where players are not only athletes but also essential components of a greater goal by promoting self-control, diligence, and dedication to team success. Numerous teams have been motivated to follow its example, and it has made the Miami Heat a model NBA team. The league's coaching methods and team relationships are still influenced by "Heat Culture," which is now acknowledged as a standard for excellence.

When considering Riley's legacy, it is impossible to ignore his leadership and mentoring contributions. He has influenced both the coaches who trained under him and the players he coached. His influence on players like Erik Spoelstra serves as an example of how leadership can be developed and transmitted, improving the game overall. As a current championship-winning coach, Spoelstra exemplifies the values Riley taught and shows that mentoring is essential to long-term basketball success.

Riley's impact is also seen in the NBA's larger business and cultural spheres outside of the court. His knowledge of fan interaction and brand development has revolutionized the way teams communicate with their communities. Riley has helped the NBA become a worldwide sensation by valuing fan interactions and creating a feeling of community, demonstrating how sports can bridge divides and unite people.

The core of Pat Riley's contributions to basketball will remain the same as we move forward. His unwavering dedication to team culture, creative teaching techniques, and unrelenting pursuit of greatness serve as a model for CEOs, coaches, and athletes alike. His leadership and vision helped shape the game's development, which will continue to motivate upcoming generations to aim high, work hard, and dream big.

Pat Riley is a legendary person in basketball history—a real visionary who has influenced the sport and motivated innumerable players. His legacy will surely last for many years to come, and his talents have helped the NBA become what it is today. As we consider his career, we are reminded that basketball greatness is about more than simply winning championships or breaking records; it's also about the enduring influence one person can have on other people's lives and the sport's culture. Pat Riley's narrative is proof of the strength of fortitude, vision, and leadership, guaranteeing that his impact will last for many generations within the league.

www.ingramcontent.com/pod-product-compliance
Lightning Source LLC
Chambersburg PA
CBHW070115230526
45472CB00004B/1261